dope

dope

THE 200 MOST AWESOME THINGS ABOUT WEED

i.m. stoned

Adams Media

New York London Toronto Sydney New Delhi

Adams Media
An Imprint of Simon & Schuster, Inc.
57 Littlefield Street
Avon, Massachusetts 02322

For information about special discounts for bulk purchases, please contact Simon & Schuster Special Sales at 1-866-506-1949 or business@simonandschuster.com.

The Simon & Schuster Speakers Bureau can bring authors to your live event. For more information or to book an event contact the Simon & Schuster Speakers Bureau at 1-866-248-3049 or visit our website at www.simonspeakers.com.

Cover design by Frank Rivera.
Cover image © iStockphoto.com/svanhorn/billnoll; pauljune/123RF.

Interior images © iStockphoto.com/daver2002ua/browndogstudios/KeithBishop/naelnabil/Hollygraphic; pauljune/123RF.

Manufactured in the United States of America

10 9 8 7 6 5 4 3 2 1

Library of Congress Cataloging-in-Publication Data
Stoned, I.M.
  Dope / I.M. Stoned.
    pages cm
  ISBN 978-1-4405-8622-4 (pb) -- ISBN 1-4405-8622-5 (pb) -- ISBN 978-1-4405-8623-1 (ebook) -- ISBN 1-4405-8623-3 (ebook)
  1. Marijuana--Humor. 2. Marijuana--Miscellanea. I. Title.
  PN6231.M24S76 2015
  818'.602--dc23

                              2014038754

ISBN 978-1-4405-8622-4
ISBN 978-1-4405-8623-1 (ebook)

Contains material adapted and abridged from *Weed 2014 Daily Calendar* by I.M. Stoned, copyright © 2013 by Simon & Schuster, Inc., ISBN 10: 1-4405-6499-X, ISBN 13: 978-1-4405-6499-4; and *Weed 2015 Daily Calendar* by I.M. Stoned, copyright © 2014 by Simon & Schuster, Inc., ISBN 10: 1-4405-7936-9, ISBN 13: 978-1-4405-7936-3.

Introduction

There's never been a shortage of self-proclaimed stoners willing to tell you why marijuana is the single greatest substance in the known universe—for hours if you'll listen. But nowadays, it's not just hippies and burners waxing poetic about the wonder drug; it's professional athletes, lawyers, actors, musicians, parents, and even doctors. For the first time in history, everyone is starting to come to terms with the fact that the stoners have been right all along: marijuana is dope.

Today we live in a nation where 58 percent of the population is in favor of legalizing marijuana. Where we once had a leading doctor insisting marijuana turned him into a bat (seriously, I couldn't make that up), we now have physicians using marijuana to effectively treat dozens (and possibly hundreds) of ailments ranging from glaucoma and Crohn's Disease to epilepsy and cancer. Perhaps more importantly, we now realize that it's entirely possible to enjoy the occasional joint and still be a productive, responsible member of society.

Whether you are a proud, self-proclaimed stoner or you can't tell the difference between a bong and a snorkel, chances are you are holding this book because you want to learn more about pot. And I can certainly promise that you will. From the history of the world's oldest weed stash to Martha Stewart's appreciation for a well-rolled joint, and everything in between, *Dope* celebrates cannabis, whether it's used to treat illness or to enhance a night spent on the couch listening to Pink Floyd. And both applications are equally wonderful.

It Gets Voters to the Polls

Healthcare reform and education bills just aren't interesting enough to get people to turn out on Election Day. Marijuana legalization, however … that's another story. When an initiative to legalize marijuana hit the Washington state ballot in 2012, voter percentage was up by around 40 percent compared to the average for the rest of the nation.

"WHY IS MARIJUANA AGAINST
THE LAW? IT GROWS NATURALLY
UPON OUR PLANET. DOESN'T
THE IDEA OF MAKING NATURE
AGAINST THE LAW SEEM TO YOU
A BIT ... UNNATURAL?"

—BILL HICKS, AMERICAN COMEDIAN

A Use for Stems Finally Discovered

The presence of the occasional stem in a bag of otherwise pristine buds is an unfortunate reality for the cannabis community, but it need not be an entirely unwelcome one. While you shouldn't smoke stems, you can harvest the THC-laden trichomes by freezing the stems and then shaking them in a jar.

Legalization Could Drop Prices by 99 Percent

Compared to other illegal drugs, marijuana is relatively inexpensive, but if it is ever legalized on the federal level it could drop to mind-blowingly low levels. Some experts believe the production cost could drop from a current estimate of $100 an ounce to as little as sixty-two cents. This could make the final cost to consumers just $3 an ounce—a staggering 99 percent drop.

"I USED TO SMOKE MARIJUANA. BUT I'LL TELL YOU SOMETHING: I WOULD ONLY SMOKE IT IN THE LATE EVENING. OH, OCCASIONALLY THE EARLY EVENING, BUT USUALLY THE LATE EVENING—OR THE MIDEVENING. JUST THE EARLY EVENING, MIDEVENING, AND LATE EVENING. OCCASIONALLY, EARLY AFTERNOON, EARLY MIDAFTERNOON, OR PERHAPS THE LATE-MIDAFTERNOON. OH, SOMETIMES THE EARLY-MID-LATE-EARLY MORNING. . . . BUT NEVER AT DUSK!"

—STEVE MARTIN, AMERICAN ACTOR

Even Low-Income Stoners Can Score Primo Bud

In 2014, the Berkeley City Council voted unanimously to force medical marijuana dispensaries in the city to distribute 2 percent of the cannabis they sell each year to low-income patients, free of charge.

You Can Grow Pot
on Your Phone

In the spring of 2014, the number one game in the Apple App Store didn't have anything to do with flying birds or candy puzzles. Instead, iPhone and iPad users were going nuts for Weed Firm, an app that allowed users to cultivate and sell marijuana from the safety of their mobile devices. The game, which many likened to the popular Grand Theft Auto series, was eventually pulled from the store by Apple despite its immense popularity.

Weed Can Boost Hamburger Sales

While the 2004 film *Harold & Kumar Go to White Castle* did wonders for the careers of the actors who played the perpetually stoned, burger-fiending title characters, it was an even bigger boon for the restaurant itself. Shortly after the film's release, sales of White Castle's delectable sliders increased by more than 10 percent. Although White Castle did not pay for the product placement, the company did embrace the film's stoner message with collectible cups and signs throughout its various locations.

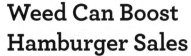

The Munchies Are a Sound Investment

Two weeks before Colorado voters passed Amendment 64, which legalized marijuana use in the state, Denver Broncos quarterback Peyton Manning purchased twenty-one Papa John's pizza franchises. However, the football star did not explicitly state that his business decision was in any way influenced by the impending change to the law.

It Keeps the USPS in Business

Most Americans can't remember the last time they received a handwritten letter, let alone sent one. Yet somehow, the United States Postal Service remains in business. One explanation could be the aid of a national network of marijuana enthusiasts sending cannabis care packages back and forth. Since 2007, seizures of marijuana by the USPS, concealed in everything from cans of beans to power tools, have increased by 400 percent.

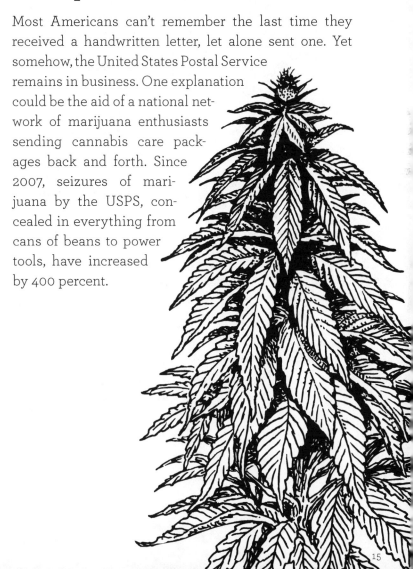

Marijuana Jump-Started eCommerce

Long before the days of Amazon and eBay, a group of computer-savvy students at Stanford University set up the first eCommerce transaction on the infant version of the Internet, dubbed ARPANET. Their first order of business was to contact students at MIT about the purchase of an undisclosed quantity of marijuana.

Weed Can Lead You to True Love

It seems there's a niche dating site for every group of people imaginable, so it's no surprise that there's even one for lovelorn stoners. Similar to sites like Match.com and OkCupid.com, 420singles.net bills itself as "420 friendly dating for singles who enjoy the freedom and benefits of Cannabis and or support its legalization."

"JUST HIT THE BLUNT ONE TIME AND SEE IF IT DOESN'T CHANGE YOUR PERCEPTION ON WHAT'S IMPORTANT IN YOUR LIFE."

—KATT WILLIAMS, AMERICAN COMEDIAN

Your Drug Dealer Might Grow Up to Be Famous

Everyone knows that rapper Snoop Lion (formerly Snoop Dogg) and actress Cameron Diaz are both advocates of marijuana use, but not everyone is aware that the two grew up together and attended the same high school. Although she is not 100 percent clear on the details, Diaz even claims to have purchased marijuana from Snoop at some point in her youth. Snoop is also hazy on the matter but confirms her claim, saying, "I might have sold her some of that white girl weed."

You Can Make a Bong Out of Snow

If you find yourself coughing up a lung every time you take a bong hit, it might be the temperature of the smoke that's causing the problem. One surefire way to cool it down is to stuff the chamber of your bong with snow or shaved ice. The snow will quickly cool the smoke as it moves up the chamber and into your lungs. For the complete icy experience, some enterprising stoners have been known to craft an entire bong out of snow.

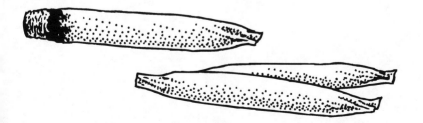

Getting High Can Be an Exact Science

For most people, smoking marijuana isn't an exact science, but it can be if that's what you want. Every time you get high, keep a journal with information like the strain you used, how much you ingested, what method you used, how high you got, and any other relevant information. After a while, you should be able to accurately replicate a particular experience by keeping certain variables consistent.

"LOOK, I HAVE NEVER MADE A SECRET OF THE FACT THAT I HAVE TRIED MARIJUANA . . . ABOUT 50,000 TIMES."

—BILL MAHER, AMERICAN TELEVISION PERSONALITY

Apocalypse Survivors Will Still Have Pot

In the event of an asteroid collision or nuclear holocaust, surviving humans can take comfort in the fact that their need for recreational marijuana has been taken into account. Scientists at the Svalbard Global Seed Vault in Norway have seeds from several different cannabis strains from throughout the globe safely secured in their facility, stored at 0°F to ensure delayed decay of the samples.

The NBA Looks the Other Way

Professional basketball players are subjected to frequent drug tests during league play as well as in the off-season. Aside from performance-enhancing drugs like steroids, off-season tests also screen for illegal narcotics—well, most of them anyway. While players are not permitted to use marijuana during the season, the NBA does not screen players for THC in the off-season.

Hemp Defeated the Nazis

During World War II, the U.S. government produced a propaganda film entitled *Hemp for Victory* to encourage farmers in the United States to grow hemp to contribute to the war effort. Until 1989 the government denied ever creating such a video, at which point marijuana advocate Jack Herer provided the Library of Congress with two VHS copies of the film.

You Can Make DIY Hash

Kief—a name for the loose trichomes of marijuana captured in a grinder—is packed full of THC, but it's too fine to pack into a bowl unless you compress it first. One easy way to do this is to wrap a small piece of thick paper around the top of an unsharpened pencil to create a one-inch cone at the top. Then place the desired amount of kief inside the cone and use a second unsharpened pencil to press the kief down into a small, dense puck of what is essentially hashish.

Rock and Roll Is Greater Than the Law

In 2010, AC/DC drummer Phil Rudd was found with twenty-five grams of marijuana on a boat he had moored in a New Zealand marina. A judge dropped the charges, however, on the simple grounds that a conviction would have prevented Rudd from touring with the band.

Rip a Bong and Still Win Eight Gold Medals

There's no denying that Michael Phelps is the greatest swimmer—and possibly overall athlete—to ever compete in the Olympic games. What's more impressive is that he may have been high as a kite the entire time. Shortly after winning a record-breaking eight gold medals at the 2008 Olympics, a photo of Phelps smoking an unknown substance from a large water pipe surfaced in the media. Phelps confirmed the picture was authentic and apologized for his childish antics, but never admitted to using marijuana while he was competing.

There's a Freaking Pot Cannon

Mexican police are no strangers to innovative methods for smuggling marijuana across the border into the United States, but in February 2013 they stumbled upon a first: a marijuana cannon. The device, which consisted of a long plastic pipe and a tank of compressed air, could fire packages of drugs as heavy as thirty pounds over the border.

Even Judges Don't Take Weed Seriously

In 2001, a Connecticut youth received a very lenient, albeit strange, sentence for possessing a marijuana pipe. A Springfield, MA, judge insisted the seventeen-year-old boy listen to Afroman's famous song, "Because I Got High," and write a report about the song and the dangers of smoking marijuana. He was also required to submit to random drug testing.

You Can Still Be President

Bill Clinton may have been the first president to admit to experimenting with marijuana, but he certainly wasn't the first to smoke it. Both George Washington and Thomas Jefferson cultivated hemp, and it is believed John F. Kennedy smoked marijuana to help ease severe back pain. As for Clinton's successors, George W. Bush admitted after he left office that he'd sparked up prior to becoming president, and President Barack Obama has never been shy about the numerous toking sessions in his youth.

"WHEN I WAS A KID I INHALED
FREQUENTLY. THAT WAS THE POINT."

—BARACK OBAMA, PRESIDENT OF
THE UNITED STATES OF AMERICA

Vaporizers Get You High
Without the Smoke

While the health risks of smoking marijuana are minimal, there are still many people who find the experience unpleasant. For them, vaporizing the plant has become a popular method for getting high. They use small machines called vaporizers, which work by heating the marijuana to just above the vaporization temperature of THC, around 315°F. The result is a cooler, high-inducing vapor rather than thick, dark smoke.

More High for Your Buck

Myths abound that today's marijuana is ten, thirty, or even a hundred times more potent than it was in the past. While these claims are exaggerated, there's no denying that the pot contained in a joint today is significantly more powerful. The average THC concentration in today's marijuana is roughly 10 percent, which is almost three times stronger than samples tested in 1983, which clocked in below 4 percent.

It Can Help You Find Your Sensi Center

As marijuana laws become more lax across the country, new businesses and services have arisen to cater to the growing culture. For example, 420 yoga studios—where attendees are encouraged to get high before class—are becoming increasingly popular on the West Coast as well as in several major cities where marijuana is decriminalized.

It's Literally Impossible to Overdose

According to a 1988 study, the lethal dose of marijuana was approximately 15,000 pounds consumed by an adult male within fifteen minutes. The numbers were speculative, however, as researchers were unable to induce death in any animal due to exposure to marijuana. By comparison, the lethal dose of heroin is estimated to be anywhere from 75 to 375 mg, depending on the weight of the individual.

"I WENT THROUGH ONE PERIOD WHEN I SMOKED A SURPRISING, A REALLY BREATHTAKING, AMOUNT OF GRASS ALMOST EVERY NIGHT."

—DAVID LETTERMAN, AMERICAN
TELEVISION PERSONALITY

Pot Facts Make Great Bedtime Stories

Author Ricardo Cortés believes it's never too early to start educating your children about the virtues of marijuana, and he's written a book to help parents do just that. His book, *It's Just a Plant*, follows a young girl who walks in on her parents enjoying a joint. It's full of colorful pictures and simple language depicting marijuana use as a benign activity reserved exclusively for adults.

"I KNOW YOU'RE SUPPOSED TO
TELL KIDS NOT TO DO DRUGS,
BUT, KIDS, DO IT! DO WEED!"

—KEVIN SMITH, AMERICAN FILM DIRECTOR

If It Works on Rats . . .

In a study published in the *Journal of Pharmacology and Experimental Therapeutics* in 2013, researchers gave both natural and synthetic marijuana extract to rats suffering from epileptic seizures. The results were astounding: The number of seizures experienced by the rats in a ten-hour period dropped from three to zero.

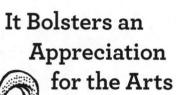

It Bolsters an Appreciation for the Arts

While classical isn't generally considered the preferred musical genre of the stoner community, members of the Colorado Symphony Orchestra hoped to change that by hosting a series of marijuana-friendly concerts in the spring of 2014. For each concert in the "High Note Series," the lucky adults who were offered invitations were encouraged to bring their own cannabis and indulge to their hearts' content while the orchestra serenaded them with pieces by Bach, Debussy, and Wagner.

Vaping Becomes Cheaper, More Portable

The first vaporizers were heavy, DIY pet projects of marijuana enthusiasts that were both expensive and cumbersome. Early retail versions were an improvement, but they cost hundreds of dollars and couldn't be used on the go. Recently, however, manufacturers have introduced pen-style vaporizers that have dropped the weight from pounds to ounces and can often be purchased for less than $100.

It's the Easiest DIY Drug

If shows like *Breaking Bad* have taught us one thing, it's that making hard drugs like methamphetamine is difficult—and dangerous. Marijuana, on the other hand, just requires a green thumb and an abundance of patience. While some strains can go from seed to smokable harvest in just eight weeks, the average grow time generally hovers around four months.

Even North Koreans Can Get High

North Korea may impose strict penalties for hard drugs like heroin, cocaine, and crystal meth, but its stance on marijuana is surprisingly lenient. While it is difficult to ascertain hard facts from the reclusive country, many believe that the plant is not considered a drug at all within the borders of North Korea. Visitors to the country report fields of cannabis plants growing along roadsides and claim citizens smoke the plant freely.

"FORTY MILLION AMERICANS SMOKED MARIJUANA; THE ONLY ONES WHO DIDN'T LIKE IT WERE JUDGE GINSBURG, CLARENCE THOMAS, AND BILL CLINTON."

—JAY LENO, AMERICAN TELEVISION PERSONALITY

Your Neighbors Never Have to Know

Smoking marijuana gives off a distinct odor that can easily stink up the entire floor of an apartment building, but it is possible to smoke indoors undetected. A common tool known as a sploof—a cardboard tube stuffed with dryer sheets—traps the pungent smoke when a user exhales into it. While the sploof doesn't completely eliminate incriminating odors, it reduces them significantly.

Obama Thinks Pot's No Big Deal

When President Obama proudly declared that he "inhaled frequently" in his youth, many in the cannabis community thought it was only a matter of time before he doubled down on his pro-marijuana stance and pushed to legalize the drug on the federal level. While that hasn't occurred, he did go on to assert in 2014 that marijuana is no more dangerous than alcohol. He also added that individual users should not receive excessive jail time when "some of the folks who are writing those laws have probably done the same thing."

Pot Makes Anything Tolerable

For those unfortunate enough to contract Hepatitis C, the side effects of the treatment—such as fatigue, nausea, and muscle pain—can be devastating. A 2006 study published in the *European Journal of Gastroenterology & Hepatology* found that only 29 percent of patients completed their treatment without the aid of marijuana. Moreover, those who used grass to alleviate the side effects were almost three times more likely to complete the treatment.

You Can Convert Almost Any Food to Get You High

When people think of edible marijuana, they usually turn to tried and true sweets like pot brownies, cookies, and cupcakes. In truth, it makes little difference what foodstuffs you use to ingest your THC. As long as the dish contains oil or butter, you can replace some or all of the nonpsychedelic ingredient with the cannabis-infused version.

Even McGruff Loves Pot

In 1980, the National Crime Prevention Council debuted a cartoon dog known as McGruff to teach children to be safe and stay away from drugs. The dog was voiced in the late nineties by actor John Morales, who apparently disagreed with his cartoon persona's stance on marijuana. The actor was arrested in 2011 when police found maps in his car leading to two indoor marijuana farms containing more than 1,000 plants.

Getting High Is a Religious Sacrament

Marijuana use may be illegal in Italy, but that law does not apply to everyone. Members of the Rastafari religion are permitted to carry small amounts of marijuana for personal use, as it is considered a sacrament. The amount a Rastafarian can carry for "personal use" is relatively vague; however, a case in 2008 deemed an amount equivalent to approximately seventy joints to be permissible.

It Makes Food Smell Better

While stoners have been insisting for centuries that weed makes food better, now there's proof. In 2014, a group of scientists administered THC to several mice and exposed them to banana and almond oils. When compared to their non-dosed counterparts, the mice that were high on THC spent a considerably longer amount of time sniffing the oils.

Pot Is Three Times Less Addictive Than Cigarettes

The belief that marijuana isn't habit forming is not entirely true, but it is certainly far less addictive than many other drugs. The worst of these is tobacco, which boasts a 30 percent addiction rate among users. In comparison, the rate among marijuana users is just 10 percent.

"IS MARIJUANA ADDICTIVE? YES, IN THE SENSE THAT MOST OF THE REALLY PLEASANT THINGS IN LIFE ARE WORTH ENDLESSLY REPEATING."

—RICHARD NEVILLE, AUSTRALIAN AUTHOR

The DEA Gives Potheads a Free Pass

The Drug Enforcement Administration is probably at the top of the list of organizations you'd think would frown upon prior drug use. And that's true for the most part, but they make some exceptions for marijuana. Their website grudgingly says, "Exceptions to this policy may be made for applicants who admit to limited youthful and experimental use of marijuana."

"AMERICAN SOCIETY WAS LONG AGO MANIPULATED INTO THE PROHIBITION OF A PLANT THAT CAUSED A MILD EUPHORIA IN MOST PEOPLE WHO TRIED IT AND A SEVERE PARANOIA IN MANY WHO DIDN'T."

—DAVID NATHAN, AMERICAN WRITER

Weed Really Does Boost Creativity

Everyone has a few stoner friends who insist they just can't get the creative juices flowing without a little bud. Well, as it turns out, there might actually be something to their claims. In 2011, a group of scientists studied the link between marijuana and creativity and postulated that ingesting cannabis causes temporary symptoms resembling psychosis. As a result, the user is better able to create links between seemingly unrelated concepts, a defining characteristic of creativity.

"IF EVER I NEED SOME CLARITY OR A QUANTUM LEAP IN TERMS OF WRITING SOMETHING, WEED'S A QUICK WAY FOR ME TO GET TO IT."

—ALANIS MORISSETTE, CANADIAN MUSICIAN

Stoners Are the Real Job Creators

The legalization of marijuana in Colorado raised millions of dollars in tax revenue in a matter of months, but what many people don't realize is that it also created thousands of jobs almost overnight. In that state alone, some estimates put the number of individuals working directly in the industry at around 10,000. That's not including all of those who benefit indirectly, such as construction workers, accountants, lawyers, and restaurant owners.

The DOJ Lets It Slide

Both residents and tourists in Colorado and Washington wonder how marijuana can be illegal on the federal level, yet they can happily enjoy a fat joint without federal agents busting down the door. The answer is the Department of Justice just doesn't care—as long as the dispensaries are on the up and up. Shortly after the two states voted to legalize marijuana, Attorney General Eric Holder issued a statement claiming the DOJ would intervene only under eight circumstances, including selling marijuana to minors, having ties with gangs or cartels, or distributing other dangerous drugs.

You Get What You Pay For

Much like fine wine and spirits, marijuana has tiered offerings for even the most economical of stoners. Depending on location and availability, thrifty stoners can track down an ounce of low-grade "schwag" for as little as $101 an ounce. Top of the line name-brand bud can go for $399 or more for the same amount.

Smelling Like a Hippie Isn't a Crime

The Supreme Judicial Court of Massachusetts ruled in 2011 that the smell of burning marijuana alone did not give police probable cause to stop pedestrians or search a vehicle. In 2014, the court went one step further and added unburned marijuana to the list of odors local and state police will have to ignore.

It Flushes Out of Your System Right Quick

It's true that THC levels build up over time for habitual smokers, but for those who only partake occasionally, you'd be hard-pressed to prove it. For individuals who smoke a single joint, THC levels in the blood drop below the 50-nanogram-per-milliliter detection level of most commercial tests within twenty-four to forty-eight hours.

Smoking Pot Doesn't Equal Tax Evasion

Recreational marijuana may be illegal in forty-eight of fifty states in the United States, but that doesn't mean it's tax exempt. In twenty states, individuals who acquire marijuana illegally can still purchase a state-issued stamp and affix it to their stash. As long as an individual caught possessing marijuana has the appropriate stamps, he or she can't be charged with tax evasion, the fines for which can reach $14,000 and seven years' imprisonment in some states.

You Don't Have to Use It to Support It

Uruguayan President José Mujica was nominated for a Nobel Peace Prize shortly after legalizing marijuana, so it may come as a surprise that he has never once used the drug since his birth in 1935. Nor does he plan to, now that the drug is legal. For those who do indulge, Mujica preaches moderation.

The TSA Is More Concerned with Your 3.5-Ounce Shampoo Bottle

Because people frequently fly from the pot-safe haven of Colorado to less cannabis-friendly locales, TSA agents have seen an influx of queries on whether or not passengers can bring their pot along for the ride. Their response is pretty straightforward: "TSA security officers do not search for marijuana or other drugs." They will of course forward the matter along to local law enforcement if they do encounter a stash. However, that only occurred ten times in the first six months of legalization.

"IF THE WORDS 'LIFE, LIBERTY, AND THE PURSUIT OF HAPPINESS' DON'T INCLUDE THE RIGHT TO EXPERIMENT WITH YOUR OWN CONSCIOUSNESS, THEN THE DECLARATION OF INDEPENDENCE ISN'T WORTH THE HEMP IT'S WRITTEN ON."

—TERENCE MCKENNA, AMERICAN WRITER

You Can Get a Cannabis Spa Treatment

Even though marijuana oils won't get you high just by rubbing them on your skin, a number of massage parlors in Colorado now offer "marijuana massages" to help customers relax. During the sessions, massage therapists apply THC-laced topical oils and creams, which they claim help soothe muscle pain and relieve tension.

More Energizing Than Red Bull

One of the most prevalent stigmas surrounding marijuana is that it makes users tired, lazy, and apathetic. This is certainly true for some strains, but not all. For example, fans of Green Crack, a cannabis hybrid of sativa and indica, claim it provides a significant energy boost and allows them to focus on tasks like house cleaning and yard work, which would otherwise be extremely tedious.

If You Test Positive, You Can Blame It on Acid Reflux

Random drug tests are an unfortunate reality for many students and employees throughout the world, but even if you test positive there's a way out—provided you suffer from acid reflux. Researchers are unsure why, but the drug Pantoprazole, often prescribed to treat acid reflux, can cause a false positive for THC.

If It Hurts, Weed Can Fix It

Marijuana's ability to treat pain is widely known, but how does it fare against chronic pain disorders like rheumatoid arthritis? According to a 2011 study, wonderfully. Patients provided with Sativex—a drug derived from cannabis plants—reported significant reductions in pain, reduced inflammation, and better sleep patterns.

Barcelona Cannabis Clubs Are the New Amsterdam Coffee Houses

The Netherlands' lax views on marijuana use have long made it a stoner mecca, but Spain is rapidly becoming another premiere country for European cannabis enthusiasts. The country sports some 700 cannabis clubs—up from just forty in 2010—which exploit a provision in Spain's drug laws that permits the growing and consumption of marijuana in private settings. While membership to the clubs is required, it's often a simple matter of applying online or calling ahead.

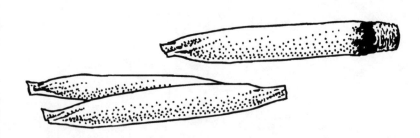

Pot Could Cure Ebola and We'd Never Know

When researching his 2013 CNN documentary *Weed*, Dr. Sanjay Gupta was shocked to discover that only 6 percent of marijuana studies conducted the previous year were focused on the medical benefits of the drug. Initially unconvinced there was a case for medicinal marijuana, Gupta had a change of heart after speaking with members of the medical community from around the world. He even went so far as to apologize in an essay for CNN titled, "Why I Changed My Mind on Weed."

"I WOULDN'T HAVE BEEN ABLE TO MAKE IT THROUGH HUNDREDS OF SHOWS IF IT WEREN'T FOR THE BENEFITS OF MEDICAL MARIJUANA."

—RUSH LIMBAUGH, AMERICAN
RADIO PERSONALITY

Don't Laugh: It Really Is a Performance-Enhancing Drug

Most people roll their eyes when athletes are disqualified for testing positive for cannabis, but there might be some truth to the claim that it gives them an unfair advantage. According to the *American Journal of Sports Medicine*, its ability to reduce anxiety, fear, depression, and tension when taken in low doses could result in superior performance among athletes. The fact that it is a banned substance certainly doesn't stop the pros, however, as it remains the second most detected performance-enhancing drug behind steroids.

"SMOKING'S A WAY TO LET YOU DOWN SLOWLY FROM A BALLGAME. IT ALSO MAKES YOU USE LESS OF THE RESOURCES AROUND. IT MAKES PEOPLE BETTER IN THE WAY THEY ACT TOWARDS SOCIETY. EVERYBODY'S NICER. IT'S HARD TO BE MEAN WHEN YOU'RE STONED."

—BILL LEE, AMERICAN BASEBALL PLAYER

There Will Always Be New Weed Lingo

If there's one thing stoners love to do, it's invent terminology to refer to marijuana, the act of smoking it, or those who appreciate it. One recent addition to that vernacular is the term "ent," which was popularized on the social news aggregation site, reddit. The term refers to individuals who enjoy consuming cannabis, and is derived from the tree-like race of Ents in J.R.R. Tolkien's Lord of the Rings series. Self-identified ents frequently refer to "trees" as a euphemism for marijuana itself.

But Uruguay's So Far!

In late 2013, Uruguay became the first country to fully legalize the sale and use of recreational marijuana. The new law limited cannabis enthusiasts to 1.4 ounces per month, and insisted the drug be purchased from licensed pharmacies by customers eighteen or older. The law also entitled citizens to grow up to six marijuana plants in their home.

You Can Still Be a Good Parent

Stoners depicted in Hollywood are missing lots of things: good hygiene, motivation, fashion sense, and even moderate levels of intelligence. But perhaps the most notable omission is children. To dissolve the notion that enjoying marijuana and being a good parent are mutually exclusive, a group of women in Beverly Hills formed "Marijuana Moms." The group meets regularly to share cannabis recipes and discuss parenting tactics, and its members argue that toking up is no worse than the occasional glass of wine enjoyed by many of their critics.

You Can Eat More Than You Ever Dreamed Possible

One of the most common uses for medical marijuana is to increase appetite for patients who have trouble eating. The reason it works so well has very little to do with the stomach, however, and a lot to do with the brain. When you eat and become full, your body produces an appetite-suppressing hormone called Leptin, which binds to cannabinoid receptors in the brain to alert you to stop eating. When you ingest marijuana and THC reaches the brain, it binds to those same cannabinoid receptors and blocks the Leptin, effectively removing the connection between your brain and stomach.

Beer and Weed Are Distant Cousins

Next time you take a sip of a nice, refreshing IPA, take a moment to appreciate the unique aroma and flavor. Notice anything familiar? Grassy undertones, reminiscent of a freshly lit joint? Those are the hops you are detecting—an essential ingredient in beer that happens to be in the Cannabaceae family of flowering plants, along with marijuana and hackberries.

Drug Dealer Is Great on a Resume

After serving ten years in prison for smuggling an estimated seventy-five tons of marijuana into the United States, Brian O'Dea took out a classified ad in Canada's *National Post* looking for legitimate work. He cited his experience running a $100 million drug business as his primary qualification, and received nearly 600 job offers.

If You Studied Stoned, You Can Take the Test Stoned

Thanks to a phenomenon known as "state dependent learning," it's not a good idea to study for a test or prepare for a presentation while under the influence of marijuana, unless you also intend to take your test or give your presentation while you are stoned. Studies have shown that subjects performed better on memory recall tasks if they were high while memorizing and when asked to recall the information. However, they performed significantly worse if they were sober during just one of the two steps.

Washington Cops Distribute Munchies Instead of Tickets

Rather than greeting cannabis enthusiasts with handcuffs and citations, Seattle police took a more welcoming approach at the 2013 Hempfest: They passed out Doritos. During the annual celebration, police distributed an estimated 1,000 bags of chips, each affixed with a sticker explaining the specifics of the state's new recreational marijuana law.

A Synthetic Version
Is Already Legal

Marijuana may still be illegal in the United States (at least at the federal level), but a synthetic version of the active chemical tetrahydrocannabinol (more commonly known as THC) is sold as a prescription drug called Marinol. The drug is FDA approved and is prescribed to treat weight loss in patients with AIDS and the nausea and vomiting that often occur following chemotherapy.

Martha Stewart Appreciates a Properly Rolled Joint

During an interview with Andy Cohen on Bravo in 2013, Martha Stewart critiqued the joint-rolling abilities of some youths she had passed on her way to the interview, describing their joint as "sloppy." The renowned homemaker immediately followed up with, "Of course I know how to roll a joint."

Weed Helps Fight the Cocaine Industry

In 2013, Colombia was faced with an epidemic of homelessness and addiction surrounding a cocaine derivative known as basuco. The drug—a smokable extract similar to crack—is very addictive and often contains residue from solvents like kerosene used to manufacture it. To solve the problem, officials in their capital city of Bogotá took a controversial approach: They provided addicts with marijuana as an alternative.

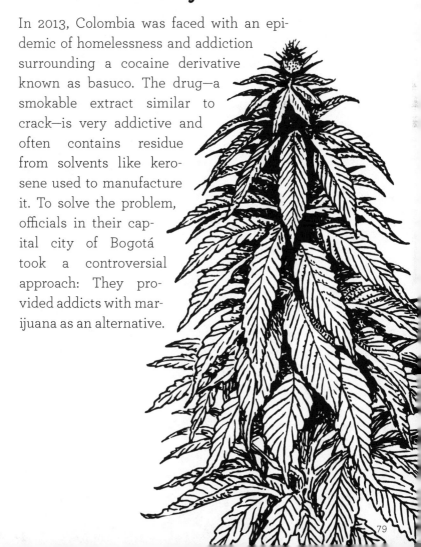

You Can Use It As an Excuse to Eat Healthy

If you find yourself binging on fatty foods like cookies, chips, and pizza whenever you get high, try to force healthier eating habits on your stoned self. Before you smoke, remove any unhealthy foods from your house or apartment and replace them with fresh vegetables, fruit, and healthy snacks like rice cakes. You'd be surprised how satisfying a fresh kiwi can be compared to a donut.

THC Keeps Pesky Herbivores Out of Your Garden

Scientists believe the chemical THC first evolved as a means for marijuana to ward off herbivores. Due to its psychoactive properties, animals that ingested the plant would become disoriented and avoid eating it in the future.

Court Rules: Pot Better Than Science

The first official medical marijuana patient in the United States was twenty-eight-year-old Robert Randall, who suffered from debilitating glaucoma. In 1976, he was charged with illegally cultivating marijuana, but he argued that his growing operation was a necessity as no other drug could halt the progress of his disorder. The court ruled in his favor and the charges were dropped. He was also allowed to receive marijuana from the government to treat his disorder.

Think of Pot As Super Potent Chocolate

While there are no reports of any individual ever getting high off of chocolate, the ubiquitous treat does contain chemicals more commonly associated with marijuana: cannabinoids. In order to get high, however, you'd have to consume a mind-blowing twenty-five pounds of dark chocolate.

Marijuana Is a Great Truth Serum

In the early 1940s, members of the Office of Strategic Services (OSS) experimented with a number of chemical compounds in search of a "truth serum" that would force a prisoner to divulge valuable information. Of all the chemicals they tested, concentrated THC proved the most useful. After the OSS administered the drug to mafia henchman Augusto Del Gracio, the formerly tight-lipped enforcer opened up about his boss's heroin trafficking but quickly realized his mistake, saying, "Whatever you do, don't ever use any of the stuff I'm telling you."

You Don't Have to Get High Every Day

The archetypical stoner portrayed in television and film seems to think of nothing but when and where to smoke the next joint. In reality, the vast majority of pot smokers partake far less often. Only about 20 percent of marijuana enthusiasts smoke every day, while between 40 and 50 percent claim to have indulged fewer than twelve times in their entire lives.

You Can Be High and Still Win an Academy Award

Before attending the 1991 Academy Awards, actress Whoopi Goldberg decided to calm her nerves with a harmless joint. While this seemed like a good idea at the time, she immediately regretted the decision when she won the award for best supporting actress for her role in the film *Ghost*. According to Goldberg, she had to mentally coach herself up the stairs and through the process of picking up the statue.

Hate Smoking? You Can Eat Your Pot

The most popular method for ingesting marijuana is to smoke the plant matter, but this is by no means the only method. Because THC is oil-soluble, it is possible to infuse oil or butter with the psychedelic chemical by adding marijuana and gently heating the mixture. The result is a high-inducing ingredient you can use to make any number of baked goods or savory dishes.

It Melts the Pain Away

Because there are surprisingly few studies focused on the medical benefits of marijuana, doctors are forced to rely on anecdotal evidence to evaluate the effectiveness of the drug. But that evidence is promising. For example, patients at the Compassionate Care Foundation dispensary in Egg Harbor Township, NJ, were asked to rank their pain before and after receiving their prescribed dosage of marijuana. Of the 145 patients who completed the survey, about 80 percent saw their pain levels decrease significantly. On average, patients claimed their pain levels dropped by 30–50 percent.

Teenage Stoners Grow Up to Rule Winterfell (Albeit Briefly)

Alfie Allen is best known as the actor who plays Theon Greyjoy in the popular HBO series *Game of Thrones*, but many of his fans are not aware that he is also the brother of British pop singer Lily Allen. She even wrote a song for him, titled "Alfie," in which she chastised him for sitting around in his room all day smoking pot.

Legalization Lowers Crime Rates

Opponents of legalization often claim that allowing recreational marijuana use will lead to drastic increases in crime rates. Once data started coming in from the great marijuana legalization experiment known as Colorado, however, that argument quickly disintegrated. In fact, since legalization Denver has seen both violent and nonviolent crimes fall by 6.9 percent and 11.1 percent respectively.

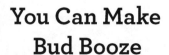

You Can Make Bud Booze

It is widely known that you can infuse butter and oil with THC, but what many don't realize is that you can do the same with alcohol. Heating marijuana in the oven to release the THC and then soaking it in a high-ABV spirit results in a potent alcohol/marijuana hybrid colloquially known as "Green Dragon."

High Times Dabbles with Hard Drugs, Decides Pot Is Best

When Steven Hager became editor of *High Times* magazine in 1988, he implemented a number of changes to the publication. Most notably, he focused the articles almost entirely on cannabis and moved the magazine away from harder drugs like heroin and cocaine. He is also credited with creating the Cannabis Cup, an awards ceremony that recognizes excellence in particular strains and products.

Contact High Is a Myth; It's Safe to Smoke Around Strangers

The vast majority of THC is absorbed by the lungs within seconds of inhaling, so the likelihood that you could get high from inhaling a passing puff of smoke is almost nonexistent. Even in confined spaces, the only way individuals who aren't directly toking up are going to get high is if they burn the bud like incense.

You Can Toke Up on Live Television

After the success of the film *Pineapple Express*, producers at the MTV Movie Awards thought it would be funny if the film's two main actors, Seth Rogen and James Franco, incorporated marijuana into their award presentation. The actors agreed, but missed a very important last-minute piece of stage direction: They weren't supposed to smoke it. The cameraman managed to cut away when the stoner duo lit up, but they can still be heard, ". . . not really smoking a big fatty joint from this giant bag of fake weed live on television right this second."

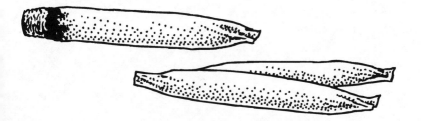

You're Never Too Old to Start Smoking Pot

Despite his claim to fame as creator of the iconic stoner duo Jay and Silent Bob (as well as their comic book personas, Bluntman and Chronic), director Kevin Smith did not start smoking pot until age thirty-eight—a full fourteen years after his first film featuring the pair of drug dealers. He was first introduced to the wonder drug by none other than Seth Rogen.

You Can Create Pot from Thin Air

Even if you've never seen a joint, you are probably familiar with hydroponics—a method of cultivation whereby plants grow in nutrient-rich liquid instead of soil. But another method, dubbed aeroponics, is not as widely known. Growers hang the plants in the air and periodically spray them with nutrients. The increased exposure to oxygen allows the plants to grow faster than with other growing methods.

Marijuana References Are Hidden in Harry Potter

The term "muggle," popularized in the popular Harry Potter series of children's books, refers to "non-magic folk." But the word's origins date back much further and are steeped in marijuana culture. In 1920s New Orleans jazz culture, the word "muggle" referred to both marijuana and to those who smoked it.

Cutest Strain Name Ever

At just six years old, Charlotte Figi may have been the youngest person to get her own marijuana strain. Charlotte suffered from Dravet Syndrome, which caused her to experience frequent and debilitating seizures hundreds of times a week. After trying countless medications, her parents turned to cannabis and the results were uncanny. To cater to her needs, a group of six Colorado brothers developed Charlotte's Web, a low-THC strain that reduced her seizures to just three a week.

Weed Keeps Electric Companies in Business

While indoor marijuana growers make up a very small percentage of the United States population, they account for an astronomical amount of energy consumption. Annually, they consume enough electricity to power 2 million American homes, approximately 1 percent of annual consumption for the entire country. Most of this energy use comes from high-intensity grow lights, which are approximately 500 times stronger than a reading lamp.

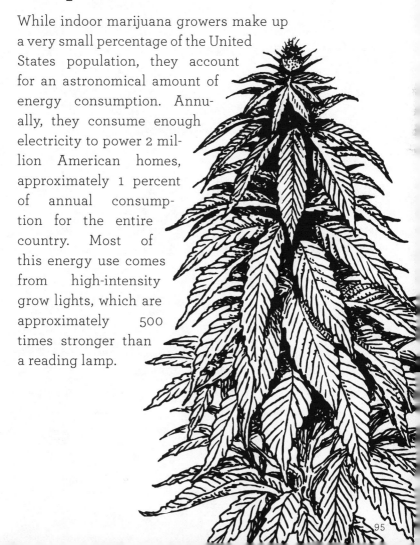

It's Not Illegal If It's a Gift

Shortly after marijuana became legal in Colorado, residents of the state began stretching the limits of the new amendment. While selling marijuana remained illegal for private citizens, adults were permitted to gift up to an ounce of marijuana, provided they did so "without remuneration." This led to a number of questionable Craigslist ads offering free marijuana while simultaneously soliciting donations for things like "rent" and "electricity."

There's a Reason It's Called Weed

With all the talk of hydroponics, nutrition packs, and heat lamps, many people forget that marijuana is an incredibly hardy plant that has grown in the wild without human intervention for eons. So hardy, in fact, that it took Australian authorities nine years to eradicate a twelve-square-mile wild crop found near Sydney in 1963.

Both Sides of the Aisle Want Legalization

Marijuana legalization has traditionally been associated with lefty liberal hippies, but even members of the GOP are beginning to hop on the cannabis bandwagon. In July 2014, house republican Dana Rohrabacher came out in favor of legalization in California. The congressman said he would likely support a bill to legalize the drug in the state in 2016, and condemned the current prohibition status quo as "totally contradictory to what our country is all about."

You Can Make Foolproof Cannabutter

If you are worried about burning your cannabutter, you can add a few cups of water to the melted butter before adding your cannabis. Once the water/butter mixture starts to boil, you can add the cannabis. Because THC is not especially water-soluble, very little of the precious chemical will leech into the water. When you are done, refrigerate the mixture until the butter rises to the top and hardens. You can then simply remove it from the water and enjoy.

Even the Residue Gets You High

Grinding marijuana makes it easier to work with when rolling joints, but it also has an oft-overlooked fringe benefit. After the marijuana has been pulverized in the grinder, a fine residue of THC-laden trichomes known as kief accumulates at the bottom. Over time, this byproduct can be harvested and pressed into a small, potent disk or sprinkled into a joint.

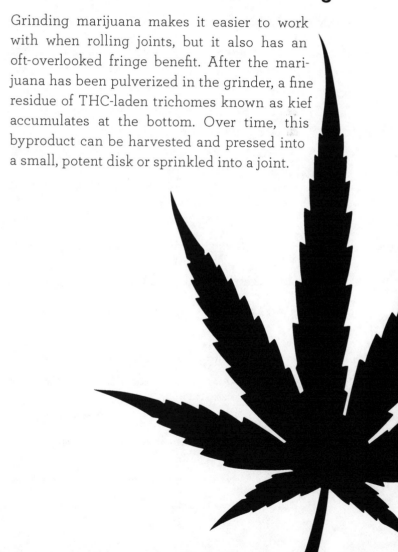

The Fine Is Less Than Jaywalking

If you are worried about winding up in prison for indulging your cannabis habit, you might be pleasantly surprised once you look up your local marijuana laws. For example, the fine for possessing up to 25 grams of marijuana in New York City is a mere $100. By comparison, jaywalking could put you $250 in debt to the city.

Marijuana as Good As Money in Hollywood

The chilling narration at the beginning of the 1974 film *The Texas Chainsaw Massacre* comes courtesy of none other than *Night Court*'s John Larroquette. The intro is less than a minute long, so Larroquette felt only a small payment was in order. For his trouble the director paid him with a single marijuana joint.

A DIY Grow Room Can Cost Less Than $1,000

While it's true you can easily drop tens of thousands of dollars building a greenhouse to produce your own pot, it's quite possible to construct a respectable grow room for a fraction of that price. If you keep the space small (around 4' × 4'), use soil instead of complicated hydroponics, go with cheaper fluorescent lighting, and cut a few corners here and there, you can start harvesting your own smokable buds in a matter of months for less than $1,000.

Discover the Cosmos with Carl Sagan

After his death in 1996, it was discovered that world-renowned astrophysicist Carl Sagan authored an essay advocating for marijuana legalization in 1969 under the pseudonym Mr. X. In the piece, Sagan described how using cannabis improved his appreciation of the arts, food, and even sex.

It Makes for a Great Band Name

Members of the popular band Green Day aren't so much huge fans of the color as they are of pot. Their original name was Sweet Children when they formed in 1987, but they dropped it in 1988 to avoid confusion with another local band, Sweet Baby. They chose the name Green Day due to their shared appreciation for marijuana. Other not-so-subtle cannabis-supporting bands include Bongwater, High on Fire, Kottonmouth Kings, and Bongzilla.

Confusing Laws Often Benefit Stoners

While marijuana may be technically illegal in the state of Alaska, residents are entitled to possess less than one ounce of the drug for personal consumption on their own property. They are also permitted to grow up to twenty-four plants for personal use. This is because of a 1975 court decision that determined the right to privacy outweighed the state's desire to ban the drug. Sale of marijuana is still illegal, however.

It Fueled the Greatest Concert of All Time

Woodstock is practically synonymous with sixties hippie culture, so it's no surprise that marijuana was readily available at the event. But just how available is impressive, even for the Flower Power generation. During the three days of peace and music, an estimated nine out of every ten concertgoers indulged in some form of marijuana consumption. And Woodstock was attended by 400,000 people.

The Government Will Deliver It to You

Despite the illegality of marijuana consumption throughout most of the United States, four individuals receive regular deliveries courtesy of the United States government. They are enrolled in the Investigational New Drug program, which allows some citizens access to medicinal marijuana. The program stopped accepting new participants in 1992, but these lucky four were grandfathered in. The marijuana is grown at the country's only government-sanctioned marijuana farm, housed at the University of Mississippi.

You Can Make a DIY Scale

If you find yourself without a scale but still need to portion out your marijuana for one reason or another, you can easily craft one with a pencil and ruler. Place the pencil on a flat surface and balance the ruler on it like a seesaw. You can then place your marijuana on one end of the ruler and an object of known weight on the other. Some helpful weights for reference: Paperclip = 1.4 grams. Penny = 2.5 grams. Nickel = 5 grams.

Robots Will Deliver Pot to You in Prison

In August 2014 authorities found a disabled drone outside of Lee Correctional Institution in South Carolina. Along with several cell phones and packages of cigarettes, the drone's payload included a substantial amount of marijuana. While not the first remote-controlled vehicle to be used to smuggle contraband into a prison, this particular drone was one of the most sophisticated ever confiscated.

It Probably Won't Give You Cancer

When scientists at the University of California set out to study a potential link between smoking marijuana and lung cancer, they expected the results to be similar to those found with cigarettes: The more you smoke, the higher your chances of getting cancer. What they found was no such connection and instead, even some indication that the drug actually prevented cancer to a small degree.

A Stoned Subject Is a Happy One

During Britain's occupation of India in the nineteenth century, British colonists were so concerned with the widespread use of marijuana among the population that they commissioned a large-scale study. After conducting interviews and testing thousands of citizens over several years, the group concluded that the drug was mostly harmless and also so ingrained in the culture that it would be impossible—and potentially dangerous—to outlaw it.

You Can Make a Pipe Out of Anything

Fancy glass pipes and bongs may be nice to look at, but they're also expensive. The good news is that there are plenty of cheap—or even free—common objects that you can modify to toke from. Our ancestors crafted pipes using everything from animal bone and antlers to wood and corncobs, but modern day DIY stoners generally prefer apples and soda cans.

Don't Know What to Smoke? There's an App for That

In 2010, web developers Scott Vickers, Brian Wanso-lich, and Cy Scott noticed a lack of comprehensive information on the hundreds of different strains of marijuana available to consumers. To fill the void, the three friends created Leafly, a website and mobile app that offers brief explanations of each strain, including its uses and effects, and allows users to add ratings and reviews. The site also helps connect users with dispensaries in areas where medical or recreational marijuana use is legal.

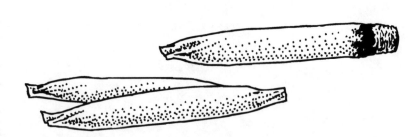

Your Encyclopedic Pot Knowledge Could Finally Pay Off

If you consider yourself a connoisseur of marijuana strains, you might have a future as a professional budtender. Similar to a sommelier at a fine restaurant, a budtender provides patrons at marijuana dispensaries with guidance when selecting strains and helps answer any questions they might have. While the starting salary is quite minimal (around $11/hour in Colorado), managers generally make around $48,000 annually.

Police Look the Other Way If You're Famous, and Naked

In 1999, Texas police were called to the home of actor Matthew McConaughey after receiving a complaint from his neighbor concerning loud music coming from his house. When they arrived, they discovered McConaughey playing his bongos and dancing around completely nude with an unnamed friend—and an undisclosed amount of marijuana. He was released nine hours later and received a $50 fine for a noise violation.

This Can Simplify Your Choices

With so many different strains of marijuana to choose from, it can be overwhelming for budding stoners to decide which is right for them. One easy way to cut through the noise is to focus on the genealogy of the strain. Species derived from the cannabis sativa plant will produce a more "heady" high, creating general euphoria and boosting creativity. Cannabis indica derivatives, however, will result in a more relaxing, full-body high.

It Makes You Hungrier, but Not Fatter

It's no secret that marijuana use increases appetite. At the same time, however, numerous studies have also found that marijuana users have fewer issues with obesity and are at a lower risk for diabetes than those who don't indulge. One recent study published in the *American Journal of Medicine* found that marijuana users have better carbohydrate metabolism, as well as lower fasting insulin levels, which could explain their ability to consume more calories yet stay thinner and healthier. Why that is the case is still a mystery.

Always Choose Natural over Synthetic

Recreational marijuana is illegal in the vast majority of states, and thankfully so are many of the dangerous synthetic alternatives. One of the most popular variants, known as K2 or Spice, allegedly caused a brother and sister to experience strokes shortly after they smoked it in 2013.

"I THINK PEOPLE NEED TO BE EDUCATED TO THE FACT THAT MARIJUANA IS NOT A DRUG. MARIJUANA IS AN HERB AND A FLOWER. GOD PUT IT HERE. IF HE PUT IT HERE AND HE WANTS IT TO GROW, WHAT GIVES THE GOVERNMENT THE RIGHT TO SAY THAT GOD IS WRONG?"

—WILLIE NELSON, AMERICAN MUSICIAN

Most Americans Acknowledge Pot's Medical Benefits

Despite the overwhelming evidence that marijuana possesses immense medical benefits, the federal government disagrees. The plant is still considered a schedule 1 drug (alongside heroin and crystal meth), which is a classification reserved for substances that have no accepted medical use. But with 73 percent of citizens in favor of legalizing medical marijuana, it seems the vast majority of Americans disagree.

"IT REALLY PUZZLES ME TO SEE
MARIJUANA CONNECTED WITH
NARCOTICS . . . DOPE AND ALL
THAT CRAP. IT'S A THOUSAND
TIMES BETTER THAN WHISKEY—
IT'S AN ASSISTANT—A FRIEND."

—LOUIS ARMSTRONG, AMERICAN MUSICIAN

Small States Can Still Get a Big High

While residents of Colorado and Washington basked in the afterglow of legal cannabis, stoners in Rhode Island silently smoked enough bowls, joints, and bongs to catapult them to the top of the usage charts. According to the 2014 National Survey on Drug Use and Health, 13 percent of Rhode Island residents over the age of twelve used marijuana monthly, making them the state with the highest percentage of stoners— almost double the national average.

Marijuana: A Vacation Destination in Itself

It didn't take long after Colorado legalized marijuana for pot-centric businesses to cash in on the budding industry (pun mostly unintended). One such organization, My 420 Tours, offers customers the opportunity to fly to the state in order to indulge in a smorgasbord of marijuana events, including dispensary tours, concerts, and workshops, all from the comfort of cannabis-friendly hotels and transportation. Packages begin at $499.

You Can Use Taxpayer Money to Fund a Colorado Weed Pilgrimage

Not long after Colorado legalized recreational marijuana use, Pennsylvania State Senator Daylin Leach took it upon himself to travel to the Rocky Mountain state to see what benefits a similar program could have in Pennsylvania. He admitted to taking a few hits from a vaporizer pen while he was there and claimed he "definitely felt something." Although the trip itself was paid for with taxpayer money, Leach insists he used his own money to purchase the marijuana.

It Kicks Cancer's Ass

Medical marijuana is often prescribed to cancer patients to help with pain management and appetite loss, but some studies suggest it could be used to treat the cancer itself. Recently, researchers in Spain applied THC directly to cancerous brain tissue and discovered that the chemical killed off the cancer cells yet left the healthy tissue intact.

It's Good for What Ails Ya

The recreational use of marijuana may be limited to just Colorado and Washington, but nearly half the states in the country allow residents some access to medical marijuana—and that number is growing. In 2014, Maryland, Minnesota, and New York all passed legislation to allow residents access to medical marijuana.

Marijuana Can Turn an Inside Joke Into an International Phenomenon

April 20 has long been an institution within the cannabis community. Each year sees countless rallies, competitions, and private smoke sessions scheduled for that day. But the genesis of "420" is rife with legends, ranging from its being the police code for marijuana smoking in progress to the number of chemicals present in the drug. The truth is that a group of high school stoners in San Rafael, CA, popularized the term in 1971 as a designated time of day when they would meet up to smoke pot.

The Manliest Man on Earth Smokes It

While the scotch-drinking, steak-eating, woodworking Ron Swanson on the popular NBC show *Parks and Recreation* doesn't smoke pot, the actor who plays him sure does. During a 2013 interview with *High Times*, Nick Offerman proudly displayed his handcrafted wooden pipe and coffin-shaped stash box packed to the brim with 100 percent pure, unadulterated marijuana. The actor had nothing but good things to say about his experience with the drug, but insisted he does not partake while filming.

Google Supports Medical Marijuana

Google normally charges a fee for ads that appear alongside popular searches, but for medical marijuana it's willing to make an exception. In July 2014, the search behemoth donated $120,000 worth of free ad space to a Michigan medical marijuana advocacy group, which used the ads to promote marijuana as a treatment for the symptoms associated with chemotherapy.

It Spans Racial and Economic Divides

While only 38 percent of U.S. adults admit to having tried marijuana, this number is remarkably consistent across demographics. Whether you make less than $30,000 annually or more than $75,000, there is a 38–39 percent likelihood that you have tried marijuana. Same goes for white individuals (at 38 percent) and nonwhite individuals (at 39 percent). No college (39 percent). Some college (40 percent). Graduate school (36 percent).

Cannabis Is More Popular Than Coffee

Shortly after the 2000 passing of Amendment 20 in Colorado, allowing the distribution of medical marijuana in the state, nearly 300 dispensaries opened up in the roughly 150-square-mile city. This meant that at least until 2011, there were more marijuana dispensaries in Denver than there were Starbucks coffee shops.

Uruguay's Pot Is Cheaper Than a Bottle of Water

While most stoners would gladly pay hundreds of dollars an ounce for the chance to smoke pot legally in Uruguay, most people are able to get high for less than the cost of a bottle of water in the United States. In an attempt to quash illegal marijuana trafficking, the government set the price at around $1 per gram, or around $28 an ounce.

The Demand for Legal Bud Is Staggering

While it should come as no surprise to any cannabis enthusiast that Colorado stoners are going through pot like hotcakes, state regulators were shocked when they crunched the sales numbers. They estimated the annual demand for cannabis in the state at around 130 metric tons. Of that, only around nine tons was consumed by tourists, with the vast majority being enjoyed by residents.

"IF I HAVE SEVEN-EIGHTHS OF
A GRAM OF WEED ON ME, I
CONSIDER MYSELF OUT OF WEED."

—RON WHITE, AMERICAN COMEDIAN

Pot Can Save You from Yourself

Any pot smoker can spend days waxing poetic about the mood-enhancing benefits of marijuana use, but hard evidence speaks louder than hard opinions. Helping lend credibility to the debate, Denver released statistics on suicide in the state following the implementation of its statewide medical marijuana program. The overall suicide rate dropped 5 percent, with an 11 percent reduction among males aged 20–29.

Smoke Young, Stay Sharp

Some researchers believe that smoking marijuana in your younger years can help stave off the onset of Alzheimer's later in life. The benefit stems from the drug's capacity to reduce inflammation all over the body—including the brain. The drug might be so helpful in this regard that overindulging in your twenties and thirties could be enough to protect you from the debilitating disease for the rest of your life.

All the Cool Kids Are Doing It

While alcohol is by far the most popular drug in the world, marijuana sits proudly atop the second-place podium. An estimated 180 million adults worldwide indulge their cannabis craving at least once a year, with about 15 percent of those being daily users.

Kids Need Medicine Too

Many parents of children suffering from epilepsy are willing to do anything to improve their children's lives—even if it means acquiring marijuana illegally to treat them. In light of the promising benefits of the drug, states like Illinois have passed new legislation allowing doctors to prescribe nonsmokable marijuana to children suffering from particular ailments, including epilepsy and other seizure disorders.

Weed Is Never "Lost," Only Redistributed

In 2008, a Japanese customs official was tasked with planting a large amount of marijuana in the luggage of an unsuspecting traveler as an exercise for the Narita airport's drug-sniffing dogs. The official lost track of the luggage, however, and the drug-sniffing dogs were unable to locate it. The airport asked any passengers who might have discovered the drugs in their luggage to return them to police, but they were never recovered. The estimated value of the wayward pot was $10,000.

Smoke It or You'll Go Blind

There currently is no cure for glaucoma, and sufferers face eventual blindness as increasing pressure buildup slowly damages their eyes. However, several studies have confirmed that regularly smoking or ingesting marijuana significantly alleviates that pressure and could help prevent blindness. The only downside is that the effects are short-lived—lasting only a few hours—so the drug must be taken several times a day. However, many would argue this is a benefit rather than a drawback.

You Can (But Shouldn't) Order Seeds Online

First and foremost, it is absolutely 100 percent illegal to purchase cannabis seeds over the Internet. It is also, in forty-eight states, absolutely 100 percent illegal to purchase and consume cannabis. That said, there is no shortage of websites, such as Weedportal.com and SeedBay.com, that will happily ship the unassuming seeds anywhere in the world, including the United States.

"THE ILLEGALITY OF CANNABIS IS OUTRAGEOUS, AN IMPEDIMENT TO FULL UTILIZATION OF A DRUG WHICH HELPS PRODUCE THE SERENITY AND INSIGHT, SENSITIVITY AND FELLOWSHIP SO DESPERATELY NEEDED IN THIS INCREASINGLY MAD AND DANGEROUS WORLD."

—CARL SAGAN, AMERICAN ASTROPHYSICIST

You Can Smoke Your Fallen Comrades

Following his tragic death in 1996, the body of rapper Tupac Shakur was cremated. Rather than keep his ashes in a ceremonial urn or scatter them in a predetermined location, members of his former group The Young Outlawz thought of a more fitting fate for his remains. According to group member Young Noble, they "...twisted up some of that great grandaddy California kush and mixed the big homie with it."

Sometimes It Falls from the Sky

In the fall of 2013, U.S. Customs and Border Protection agents were called to a field near San Diego, CA, just a few miles north of the Mexican border. When they arrived, they discovered a metal cage enclosing more than 260 pounds of marijuana, which had been dropped from a plane originating in Mexico. The massive bundle of pot was worth an estimated $157,000.

Weed Tax Could Fund Rhode Island

Despite efforts by forward-thinking states like Colorado and Washington to make smoking a joint as legal as drinking a glass of scotch, marijuana is still illegal on the federal level. But if skeptical politicians ever decide to do the math on tax revenue, that might change. A 2010 Cato Institute study estimated that legalizing the sale of recreational marijuana could generate $8.7 billion in tax revenue. That's equal to the yearly budget for the entire state of Rhode Island, or enough money to buy every adult in the country three grams of pot!

A Single Joint Can Get Hundreds of Stoners High

The largest joint ever rolled allegedly was constructed by Los Angeles resident and card-carrying medical marijuana user Brett Stone on New Year's Eve in 2006. It was reportedly three feet long and contained 112 grams of marijuana. Multiple attempts have been made since then to break the record; however, legal concerns have stopped most efforts before they even started.

"WHEN YOU SMOKE THE HERB IT REVEALS YOU TO YOURSELF."

—Bob Marley, Jamaican musician

There Are Workarounds to Purchase Paraphernalia

When purchasing paraphernalia from a head shop in areas where marijuana use is illegal, it's important not to imply that you plan to use your purchase to smoke marijuana. Instead, stick to more ambiguous terminology such as: Marijuana = Tobacco Product. Bong = Water Pipe. Bowl = Tobacco Pipe. Kief = Pollen.

You Can Roll a Joint Without Rolling

Crafting a fat, perfectly uniform joint is not so easy if you lack experience. Thankfully there's a simple alternative. Gently remove the tobacco from an unlit cigarette and slowly pack the resulting paper tube with as much bud as you'd like. Remove the filter and twist one end shut to produce a perfectly respectable joint.

Marijuana Is Not a Gateway Drug

It is true that there is a correlation between experimentation with marijuana and experimentation with harder narcotics. It is also true that there is a correlation between your feelings about mayonnaise and your dancing ability—if you like mayo, odds are you are a better dancer than your friends who don't. What both scenarios lack is a causal effect. Yet the theory persists, despite the findings of a National Academy of Sciences panel in 1999 that determined, "There is no evidence that marijuana serves as a stepping stone on the basis of its particular drug effect."

It Treats Almost Everything

Nearly everyone is familiar with marijuana's reported capacity to treat things like chronic pain, glaucoma, and nausea, but the benefits of the wonder drug could extend to as many as 200 ailments. Some lesser-known issues that could benefit from a little toke include insomnia, premenstrual syndrome, writer's cramp, and even stuttering.

There's Facebook for Marijuana

Ever wanted to show off your hand-blown glass bubbler to your stoner friends on Facebook, but didn't want your mom to see? There's an app for that. Massroots (*www.massroots.com*), dubbed the "official social networking site for the stoner community," provides users with an outlet where they can share animated gifs and pictures with other like-minded stoners. The site calls itself "an anonymous and independent social network built to connect medicinal cannabis patients." The app does not require identifying information like a name or e-mail address from its users.

You Can Smoke It Anywhere: Even the White House

While no one is certain whether a sitting president has ever gotten high at 1600 Pennsylvania Avenue, there are several people who claim to have toked up under the White House roof—and on it. In 2014, rapper Snoop Lion revealed in an interview with Jimmy Kimmel that he smoked a blunt in a White House bathroom, and Willie Nelson's biography *Willie Nelson: An Epic Life* contains a passage where Nelson smokes a joint on the White House roof during Jimmy Carter's presidency.

It Doesn't Need to Get You High

Marijuana has a number of medical benefits, and also has the fortunate side effect of getting the patient high. But for patients who want to treat their lower back pain without the psychedelic bonus, there's hope. Researchers at an Israeli medical marijuana company have developed a strain called Avidekel, which contains almost no THC but is packed full of CBD, a chemical that possesses anti-inflammatory properties but lacks THC's euphoric side effects.

Multiple Sclerosis?
Here, Smoke This

Despite its questionable legal status, sufferers of everything from gout to migraines have been self-medicating and insisting the drug helps them cope. One such group had their claims vindicated in 2012 when a study of thirty patients with multiple sclerosis found their painful symptoms significantly diminished after smoking pot. Many states that allow doctors to prescribe medical marijuana now offer sufferers of MS the option of a joint.

No More Trolling
Craigslist for Dealers

In the old days, you had to know a guy who knew a guy who knew a guy in order to score some pot. Today, there's Weedmaps. Based on Google's popular Google Maps service, Weedmaps pinpoints dispensaries and provides reviews and rankings to help you sort through the results. The site also helps users find licensed physicians and even provides suggestions on strains to use for particular ailments.

Marijuana Cultivation Is Serious Business

Just because marijuana strains sport humorous monikers like Purple Urkel, Cat Piss, and Alaskan Thunderfuck, doesn't mean the people who grow them don't take their craft very seriously. Each year, thousands of growers and enthusiasts congregate for the Cannabis Cup, where panels of judges sample and rank various strains and edibles. The event was created in 1987 by Steven Hager, the editor of *High Times* magazine, and was held in Amsterdam until 2013 when the first U.S. version was held in Denver, CO.

Legal Pot Doesn't Equal High Drivers

Groups against the legalization of marijuana often point to increases in drivers testing positive for the drug in states where medical and recreational marijuana have been legalized. While there is a correlation between the two, current drug tests merely indicate that the individual has ingested marijuana within the past few days or even weeks, not that the individual was inebriated at the time of the test. In Colorado, fatalities actually decreased in the months following the legalization of marijuana.

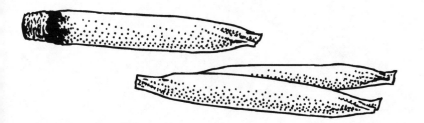

Colorado Wasn't a Fluke

When Colorado started pulling in tax money hand over fist after the state legalized marijuana, naysayers were quick to point out that success there didn't guarantee success elsewhere. Fortunately, it took only three days after Washington state opened its first recreational dispensaries to put that argument to rest. The state pulled in nearly $150,000 in tax revenue during the first seventy-two hours of sales, and projected it would earn more than $500 million within the first four years of the program.

Your Body Already Contains Similar Chemicals

Substances like marijuana are bad because they contain chemicals, and chemicals are bad, right? Wrong! Your body is chock full of naturally occurring chemicals, some of which can also be found in marijuana. For example, breast milk contains endocannabinoids, also found in marijuana, which stimulate the suckling response in newborns. Given the connection, researchers believe there could be medical applications with cannabis for pediatric conditions such as failure to thrive.

Federal Legalization Would Oust the Cartels

Despite the legalization of marijuana in Washington and Colorado, as well as the increased popularity of medical marijuana throughout the United States, the majority of pot still enters the United States courtesy of Mexican drug cartels. Some estimates put the number as high as 67 percent; however, marijuana only makes up as little as 16 percent of the cartels' revenue. The majority comes from cocaine, heroin, and methamphetamine.

The Foundation for Marijuana Fear Is Steeped in Absurdity

Americans weren't always terrified of marijuana. Prior to the 1930s, the drug was perfectly legal. It wasn't until Harry J. Anslinger joined the Federal Bureau of Narcotics that things took a turn for the worse. To lend credibility to his smear campaign against pot, Anslinger frequently referred to testimony by Dr. James Munch, whose outrageous claims included, "After two puffs on a marijuana cigarette, I was turned into a bat."

"EVEN IF ONE TAKES EVERY REEFER MADNESS ALLEGATION OF THE PROHIBITIONISTS AT FACE VALUE, MARIJUANA PROHIBITION HAS DONE FAR MORE HARM TO FAR MORE PEOPLE THAN MARIJUANA EVER COULD."

—WILLIAM F. BUCKLEY, JR.,
AMERICAN POLITICAL PUNDIT

Marijuana Kills the Unkillable

The deadly super bacteria known as MRSA hospitalizes more than 100,000 Americans every year. MRSA is particularly dangerous, as it is resistant to nearly all antibiotics and other treatment methods. However, scientists have experienced promising results with cannabinoids found in cannabis sativa. Because the cannabinoids kill bacteria differently than traditional antibiotics, scientists hope they will be able to use them to treat the infection effectively in the near future.

Dope Makes You Smarter

One of the most popular myths surrounding marijuana has always been that it kills brain cells and makes the user, for lack of a better term, dumb. In fact, several studies have found that cannabinoids actually promote brain cell growth, as well as improving mood and reducing anxiety.

"I LIKE TO TAKE A PUFF OR TWO
BEFORE GOING ON THE AIR. I
STILL GET STAGE FRIGHT WHEN I
HAVE TO PERFORM. A LITTLE GRASS
GETS RID OF THE PROBLEM."

—BOB DENVER, AMERICAN ACTOR

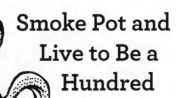

Smoke Pot and Live to Be a Hundred

Gus Ridley, star of the short documentary *A Stoner's Life*, was possibly the world's oldest stoner; he was ninety-eight during filming. He claimed to have started smoking marijuana in 1936, just one year before it became illegal in the United States.

Even a Disaster Is Bearable with Weed

Everyone remembers the plight of the thirty-three Chilean miners trapped underground for sixty-nine days in 2010 and the outpouring of food, toiletries, and magazines sent down to keep them alive and entertained. Few people know that along with all of the essentials, like food and water, several parcels of "nonessential" marijuana were smuggled down to a few lucky miners via personal family letters. The special deliveries created some tension in the group, however, as those who did not receive green care packages became jealous of their comrades.

No Two Buds Are Created Equal

There was a time when scoring pot meant tracking down your dealer and ordering, "One marijuana, please." Nowadays, however, there are hundreds of strains to choose from, offering a range of different effects. Some calm your nerves, others relax your muscles, while a few will boost your creativity or even increase your sex drive.

Weed Spawned L.A.'s Greatest Prank

On the day California's relaxed marijuana law took effect in January 1976, artist and marijuana advocate Danny Finegood modified one of the state's most famous landmarks to commemorate the event. Using a series of curtains, he changed the beloved Hollywood sign to read "Hollyweed." The prank even earned him an A for a school assignment.

Newest Generation of Vaporizers Contain NASA Tech

While there are a number of technologically impressive vaporizers on the market, the Herbalizer is the only one crafted by former NASA engineers. Inventors Josh Young and Bob Pratt took the knowledge they had gained from designing advanced NASA computer systems, and used it to create a vaporizer that heats up in less than five seconds and can be used with an inflatable bag, with a simple hose, or as a classic aromatherapy system. Unlike many vaporizers, which have preset temperatures, the Herbalizer allows users to customize their heat settings between 290°F and 445°F.

Prohibition Is a Waste of Time and Resources

Nearly half of all the individuals arrested on drug charges in 2012 were booked for incidents related to marijuana. Of those, an embarrassing 88 percent were brought in merely for possession.

"IT COSTS OVER $20,000 A YEAR
TO KEEP A POTHEAD IN PRISON.
THAT'S A LOT MORE THAN HAVING
A POTHEAD LIVE ON YOUR COUCH."

—PENN JILLETTE, AMERICAN ILLUSIONIST

Even the Beatles Were Late to the Party

Despite their iconic status as a band fueled by mind-altering substances, the Beatles actually didn't start smoking pot until 1964, just after they had risen to international stardom. Their first experience with the drug came courtesy of rock journalist Al Aronowitz and folk legend Bob Dylan. The two had wrongly assumed the band were longtime smokers, based on a mishearing of the line "I can't hide/I can't hide" as "I get high/I get high" in the song "I Want to Hold Your Hand."

Don't Fear the Bong Water

Many cannabis enthusiasts love the cooling effect bong water has on marijuana smoke, but worry that much of the precious THC leaches into the water with every hit. While it's true that THC is slightly water-soluble, the amounts lost are incredibly negligible—0.0028 milligrams of THC per milliliter of water, to be exact.

Legalization Weakens the Cartels

As states begin to adopt a more relaxed attitude toward cannabis, marijuana farmers in Mexico's infamous Sinaloa state are giving up on growing the plant altogether. Since 2009, prices for a kilogram of marijuana in the region have dropped from $100 to a mere $25.

Weed Can Benefit Your Furry Friends Too

After seeing the incredible benefits medical marijuana can have for humans suffering from chronic pain, many pet owners wonder if the drug could also work for their furry friends. Many vets believe the answer is an emphatic yes. One of the most vocal advocates for treating animals with cannabis was Doug Kramer, a Los Angeles veterinarian who first prescribed marijuana to his aging Siberian husky. She'd taken a turn for the worse after having surgery to remove several tumors, but after receiving marijuana treatments she stopped whimpering, started eating, and was able to greet him at the door again.

Sometimes Free Pot Just Appears

In September 1987, an estimated twenty-two tons of marijuana were tossed from a yacht near Rio de Janeiro after a drug deal went bad. Of the tens of thousands of two-pound cans that washed up on beaches in the ensuing weeks, only twenty were ever turned in by local residents.

Sometimes the Cops Don't Care That It's Illegal

Despite the popular belief that marijuana is 100 percent legal in the Netherlands, the Dutch have never officially legalized its sale. Instead, it has been an official policy since 1976 to ignore existing laws against possessing marijuana in small amounts or purchasing it at designated coffee shops. It is still illegal to grow or distribute marijuana in the Netherlands.

It's Less Harmful Than Alcohol and Cigarettes

In 2010, a panel of experts from the Independent Scientific Committee on Drugs set out to determine the most harmful drugs in the world. Using sixteen separate criteria for both personal and societal harm, they gave alcohol a score of 72 out of 100 on the scale, making it the most harmful drug on earth. Tobacco came in sixth just behind cocaine. Where does that leave cannabis? In eighth place, at just 21 on the harm scale.

"PEOPLE SAY YOU CAN ABUSE MARIJUANA. WELL SHIT, YOU CAN ABUSE CHEESEBURGERS TOO. YOU DON'T GO AROUND CLOSING BURGER KING."

—JOE ROGAN, AMERICAN COMEDIAN

You Can Smoke Eighty-One Blunts a Day and Still Function

During an "Ask Me Anything" question-and-answer session on the news aggregator site, reddit, in 2012, musician Snoop Lion claimed to smoke eighty-one blunts a day, seven days a week. He also confirmed that Willie Nelson was the only person to ever out-smoke him, and revealed he once went 164 days without smoking marijuana. However, he did not reveal at what point in his life he took the hiatus, or why.

You Can Get High While You Get Down

THC is oil-soluble. Lubricants are oil-based. It was only a matter of time before someone put two and two together. The resulting product, Foria, is designed as a pre-lubricant to be applied to female genitalia at least thirty minutes before arousal. Each spray contains approximately 2 milligrams of THC, and users should allow between thirty and sixty minutes for the effects to kick in.

Ignore the Hype, Aluminum Is Safe

One urban legend that surrounds DIY foil or can pipes is that smoking with aluminum can lead to Parkinson's disease. In truth, there is no confirmed link between aluminum and the degenerative neurological disorder. And even if there were, the boiling point of aluminum is roughly 4,566°F, which far exceeds the range of even the hottest commercially available lighters.

Edibles Don't Have to Be Hard

The process of making pot butter or oil can be time-consuming and rather daunting for inexperienced chefs. If you still want to eat your pot rather than smoke it, a delectable treat known as a "firecracker" might be more your speed. Simply wrap one gram of ground marijuana in a foil packet and bake it at 250°F for fifteen minutes. Spread some peanut butter on two crackers, sprinkle the baked pot on top of each, sandwich them together, wrap the cracker sandwich in foil, bake for thirty minutes at 400°F, and enjoy.

Pot Dispensaries Are Tech Savvy

Legalizing marijuana on the state level in Washington and Colorado has presented one big challenge: How do customers pay for it? With most credit card companies staying far, far away from the sale of marijuana, some dispensaries have turned to cryptocurrencies like Bitcoin to conduct sales. However, most pot purveyors still rely on cold, hard cash.

It's Cooler Than Alcohol and Cigarettes

In the eighties and nineties, booze and cigarettes were king among teens. But today's youth are anywhere from 25–50 percent less likely to drink alcohol and smoke cigarettes. Marijuana use, however, is rising steadily, with 25 percent of teens surveyed admitting to having used marijuana at least once in the last year. Many believe the shift can be attributed to an increased negative association with the dangers of alcohol and cigarettes and a belief that marijuana is less harmful.

"I HAVE CONTEMPT FOR PRETTY MUCH EVERY DRUG OTHER THAN POT. I FIND DRUNK PEOPLE GROSS. MOST PEOPLE WITH MORE THAN ONE DRINK IN THEM AREN'T GIGGLY, GOOFY, AND HAPPY THE WAY PEOPLE ARE WITH A PUFF OF POT SMOKE IN THEM ... AT A PARTY, I HAVE SO MUCH FUN STONED, FLITTING ABOUT—BUT ONCE I SNIFF THAT FIRST WAVE OF DRUNKENNESS ON SOMEONE, I'M OUT OF THERE."

—SARAH SILVERMAN, AMERICAN COMEDIAN

There's Pot Delivery for the Lazy Stoner

Adding to the already long list of marijuana-centric businesses in Colorado and Washington, a number of pot delivery services have sprung up. Often free of charge, a sales associate will arrive within the hour, marijuana order in hand. Although these unique businesses operate in a bit of a legal gray area, for now the police are choosing to look the other way.

Weed Tea: For the Sophisticated Stoner

The preferred method for brewing weed tea is to prepare a normal bag of tea and add the desired amount of premade cannabis milk. Purists who wouldn't dare befoul their mug with milk might want to try something other than steeping their weed. Due to THC's low water solubility, it would take between 8 and 12 liters of THC-infused water to deliver the necessary dose to get the drinker high.

God Will Never Give Up the Ganja. Why Should You?

Morgan Freeman might not actually be God, but he certainly has portrayed the omniscient deity in films—so that has to count for something. Regardless of his ethereal status, the Oscar-winning actor has given up cocaine and other hard drugs that he dabbled with in his youth. But ganja is with him for the long haul. When asked about his marijuana use in a 2003 interview, Freeman referred to it as God's own weed and advised, "Never give up the ganja."

"I HAVE ALWAYS LOVED MARIJUANA.
IT HAS BEEN A SOURCE OF JOY
AND COMFORT TO ME FOR
MANY YEARS. AND I STILL THINK
OF IT AS A BASIC STAPLE OF LIFE,
ALONG WITH BEER AND ICE AND
GRAPEFRUITS—AND MILLIONS OF
AMERICANS AGREE WITH ME."

—HUNTER S. THOMPSON, AMERICAN WRITER

It Makes for a Memorable Name

When trying to think of a memorable name for her daughter, Maggie Johnson felt the first name Marijuana and the middle name Pepsi would ensure she'd never struggle to stand out. Despite her controversial name, the now grown-up schoolteacher insists she has never tried the illicit drug. Marijuana also prefers orange soda.

We Can't Let the Kiwis Win

According to the 2012 United Nations World Drug Report, Australia and New Zealand contain the most marijuana smokers per capita in the world. The estimated annual usage worldwide is 2.6–5 percent; however, a staggering 9.1–14.6 percent of citizens in the two countries use marijuana each year. The majority of respondents, 61 percent, do not use any other recreational drug other than cannabis.

You Can Blame the Smell on Wolf Pee

Next time local law enforcement hassles you about that strange aroma emanating from your house, consider blaming it on a pack of South American maned wolves. The smell of this animal's urine so closely resembles marijuana that authorities were once called to the Rotterdam Zoo because a visitor standing near the maned wolf enclosure assumed someone was toking up.

It's Barely a Crime in Seventeen States

Washington and Colorado made headlines when residents voted to legalize recreational marijuana use in 2013, but they are not the only stoner safe havens in the United States. In April 2014, Maryland joined sixteen other states that have decriminalized the drug, imposing a small fine rather than jail time on individuals in possession of less than an ounce.

Seven Out of Ten Doctors Approve

In a survey conducted by the *New England Journal of Medicine* in 2013, doctors were asked whether they would prescribe medical marijuana to a hypothetical sixty-eight-year-old patient with breast cancer that had spread to her lungs, chest, and spine. Of the 1,446 doctors surveyed, 76 percent said they would approve her use of the drug.

It Made Possible the Most Important Document in U.S. History

Many stoners will be disappointed to discover that the Declaration of Independence was not, in fact, written on hemp paper. Like many important documents of the time, the final version was penned on parchment. But the first few drafts? Those were composed on pure, unadulterated Dutch hemp paper.

Ten Pounds Is Nothing When You're Bill Murray

Before his entry into acting, Bill Murray had a brief stint as a marijuana trafficker. On his twentieth birthday back in 1970, Murray was standing in line at Chicago's O'Hare airport when federal agents detained him, searched his luggage, and discovered ten pounds of marijuana valued at $20,000. He pled guilty to possession of cannabis and received five years of probation.

It's Already Super Cheap

With an average cost of $300 per ounce in the United States, getting high may seem like an expensive way to spend a Friday night. But it's actually far cheaper than most people realize. An ounce contains roughly 28 grams, which boils down to about $10 per gram. Everyone is different, but a gram is more than enough to get the average person high as a kite, and many users need less than half that amount.

Our Ancestors Got High All the Time

After an estimated 2,700 years locked in a grave in the Gobi Desert, almost two pounds of marijuana were uncovered in 2008. Tests performed on the ancient stash found it to be very similar chemically to the variety grown today, and to possess the same psychoactive properties. This cast doubt on the notion that ancient civilizations grew hemp plants strictly for making clothing and rope. Scientists believe the plant matter was ingested rather than smoked, as they found no apparatus or other paraphernalia necessary for smoking it.

Weed Makes Great Pig Food

In Bhutan, marijuana is widely abundant and is often used as a cheap source of feed for livestock. After marijuana became legal in Washington state, an intrepid butcher sought to emulate Bhutan's practices and began feeding marijuana refuse to his pigs, which are later slaughtered to make prosciutto. It is unclear whether any of the high-inducing chemicals make their way into the meat, but he does claim that the first few batches were "redder and more savory" than normal.

Marijuana Basically Prints Money

Within just a few months of legalizing recreational marijuana use, it became clear to Colorado state officials that the demand for legal bud far outpaced their expectations. In April 2014, they increased the projected tax revenue from sales of marijuana by 40 percent, up to $98 million. And where does all that money go? Along with funding marijuana education, nearly 30 percent is earmarked for improving existing education infrastructure and building new schools.

You Can Employ an Army of Bees to Protect Your Crop

When Russian police attempted to remove more than 500 marijuana plants growing near the city of Kostroma, they were forced to abandon the operation after hundreds of angry bees began an all-out assault. When questioned, a local beekeeper insisted he had nothing to do with the marijuana growing on his land, but police suspect the bees might have been placed there deliberately to protect the crop.

You Can Cut Out the Middle Man and Go Homegrown

One oft-overlooked facet of Colorado's experimentation with cannabis legalization is the fact that residents can grow their own. Residents of the state are legally entitled to cultivate up to six plants on their own property, as long as no more than three are flowering at the same time.

The Times They Are a-Changin'

A 2013 Gallup poll revealed that a clear majority of Americans favor marijuana legalization, with 58 percent being in favor. This is a starkly different response from when the group first asked the question in 1969 and only 12 percent of responders favored legalization.

Not Everything Has to Be a Pot Reference

Despite the popular myth that Peter, Paul and Mary's 1963 hit song "Puff the Magic Dragon" is a thinly veiled reference to smoking marijuana, the band insists that there are no connections to the drug. It really is just a song about a boy and his magical dragon.

Pot Brings People Together. Even Weird Ones.

When you have pot, everyone wants to be your friend. So it should come as no surprise that cannabis can even bring together two people as different as actor Johnny Depp and shock rocker Marilyn Manson. The two were spotted in early 2014 carrying a marijuana pipe while palling around shortly after Depp dropped his daughter off at school.

You Can Repurpose Spent Bud

Vaporizers are becoming increasingly popular among the cannabis community, but many vapers don't realize they are throwing away perfectly usable bud every time they empty the chamber. Because vaporizers don't actually combust the plant material, there is still a fair amount of THC present in the spent material after a vaping session. The leftover plant material can be used to make cannibutter or oil.

Edibles Are Like a Pot Time Bomb

Marijuana enthusiasts who usually inhale their THC rather than eating it should take note before chowing down on pot brownies. When inhaled, the THC in the smoke travels through the lungs, into the bloodstream, and to the brain within a matter of minutes. When ingested, however, it can take upward of an hour for the drug to take effect. This can actually work to the stoner's advantage, as he or she can consume an edible at home before a concert or other event, and it won't kick in until later.

Weed Has Its Own Police Car

In 2011, the marijuana advocacy group National Organization for the Reform of Marijuana Laws (NORML) appropriated a decommissioned police car to help further their cause. Dubbed the "Truth Enforcement Vehicle," the former squad car patrolled the Dallas-Fort Worth area spreading information about the benefits of marijuana legalization. The flashing blue and red lights were replaced with green LEDs.

The *New York Times* Thinks It's Cool

In July 2014, the *New York Times* added its two cents to the marijuana debate and emphatically declared that marijuana should be legalized on the federal level. The editorial likened the current situation with marijuana to the alcohol prohibition debacle of the twenties and thirties, but did recommend that sale of the drug should be limited to adults above the age of twenty-one.

Pot Gets Better with Time

Between 1990 and 2007, the average purity of cannabis found in the United States rose 161 percent, while the average purity of heroin and cocaine went up only 60 percent and 11 percent respectively. Marijuana is also considerably cheaper than it was in 1990, having dropped 86 percent in price.

Just in Case There's No Weed in Heaven

Bob Marley was almost as famous for his love affair with marijuana as he was for his music, so it's no surprise that he made sure to keep a little bud handy in case he needed it in the afterlife. Along with a Gibson guitar and a bible opened to Psalm 23, the Jamaican Reggae artist was buried with a small amount of marijuana.

You Control How High You Get

Taking a large hit and then holding it in the lungs to get more high may sound like an old stoner legend, but there is some truth to it. A study conducted in 1991 found that smokers who waited fourteen to sixteen seconds to exhale experienced greater THC absorption than those who exhaled after just a few seconds.

You Can Pick Some Up on Your Way to Best Buy

In 2008, law enforcement officials stumbled upon more than 200 marijuana plants growing in a makeshift greenhouse inside Miami Dade County's Mall of America. The small room came complete with a surveillance system, air conditioning, and an elaborate hydroponic growing system, and housed plants ranging from three to six feet tall. Because the plants could be harvested several times a year, police estimated their value to be several million dollars.

Is There Anything Pot Can't Cure?

Adding to the seemingly endless list of medical maladies treatable with medical marijuana, research conducted in 2013 suggests that the drug could help individuals who suffer from the inflammatory bowel disorder known as Crohn's Disease. Individuals who participated in the study smoked two joints a day for eight weeks. At the conclusion of the study, half of the subjects reported a complete cessation of their symptoms.

Printed in the United States
By Bookmasters